The INSIDE GUIDE

THE MICROSCOPIC WORLD

Cells

Under the Microscope

By Judy Thorpe

Cavendish Square

Published in 2024 by Cavendish Square Publishing, LLC
2544 Clinton Street, Buffalo, NY 14224

Website: cavendishsq.com

This publication represents the opinions and views of the author based on their personal experience, knowledge, and research. The information in this book serves as a general guide only. The author and publisher have used their best efforts in preparing this book and disclaim liability rising directly or indirectly from the use and application of this book.

Disclaimer: Portions of this work were originally authored by Maria Nelson and published as *Cells Up Close* (Under the Microscope). All new material this edition authored by Judy Thorpe.

All websites were available and accurate when this book was sent to press.

Library of Congress Cataloging-in-Publication Data

Names: Thorpe, Judy, author.
Title: Cells under the microscope / Judy Thorpe.
Description: Buffalo, NY : Cavendish Square Publishing, [2024] | Series: The inside guide. The microscopic world | Includes bibliographical references and index.
Identifiers: LCCN 2022054119 | ISBN 9781502667939 (library binding) | ISBN 9781502667922 (paperback) | ISBN 9781502667946 (ebook)
Subjects: LCSH: Cells–Juvenile literature. | Microscopy–Juvenile literature.
Classification: LCC QH582.5 .T46 2024 | DDC 571.6–dc23/eng/20221212
LC record available at https://lccn.loc.gov/2022054119

Editor: Jennifer Lombardo
Copyeditor: Danielle Haynes
Designer: Deanna Paternostro

The photographs in this book are used by permission and through the courtesy of: Cover Digital Photo/Shutterstock.com; p. 4 Sergey Kohl/Shutterstock.com; p. 6 (top) R. Hooke/Wellcome Collection; p. 6 (inset) Valery Vishnevsky/Shutterstock.com; p. 7 Kris Wiktor/Shutterstock.com; p. 8 Peter Hermes Furian/Shutterstock.com; pp. 10, 21 VectorMine/Shutterstock.com; p. 12 Dariusz Jarzabek/Shutterstock.com; p. 13 Materialscientist/Wikimedia Commons; p. 14 Designua/Shutterstock.com; p. 16 Kigsz/Wikimedia Commons; p. 18 Vladimir Staykov/Shutterstock.com; pp. 19, 29 (bottom) SciePro/Shutterstock.com; p. 22 Krakenimages.com/Shutterstock.com; p. 24 ShadeDesign/Shutterstock.com; p. 25 World History Archive/Alamy Stock Photo; p. 26 NASA/Robert Markowitz; p. 28 (top) Giovanni Cancemi/Shutterstock.com; p. 28 (bottom) Pasotteo/Shutterstock.com; p. 29 (top) Andrii Vodolazhskyi/Shutterstock.com.

Some of the images in this book illustrate individuals who are models. The depictions do not imply actual situations or events.

CPSIA compliance information: Batch #CSCSQ24: For further information contact Cavendish Square Publishing LLC at 1-877-980-4450.

Printed in the United States of America

Find us on

CONTENTS

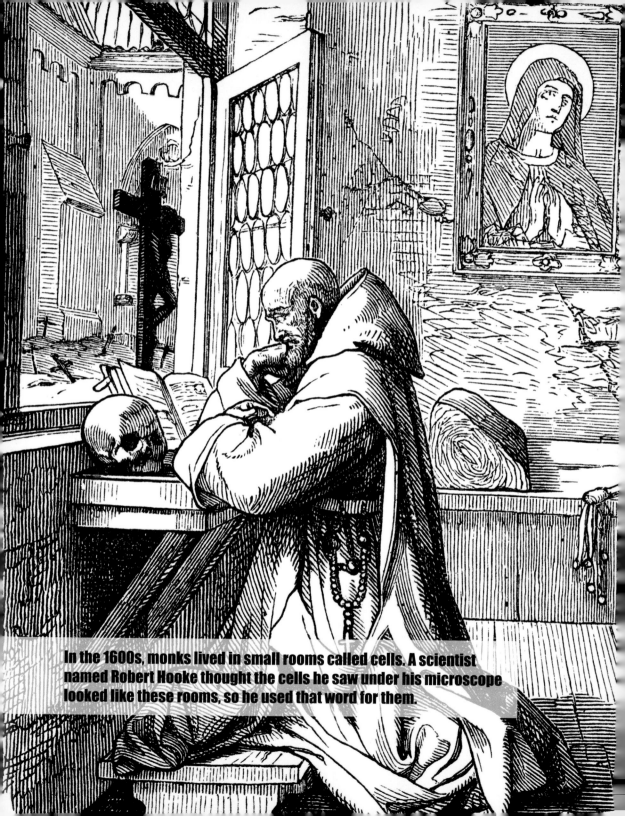

In the 1600s, monks lived in small rooms called cells. A scientist named Robert Hooke thought the cells he saw under his microscope looked like these rooms, so he used that word for them.

CELLS EVERYWHERE

It might be hard to believe, but every living thing in the world is made up of cells. **Complex** creatures, such as humans, have more than 37 trillion cells inside them. Simple ones, such as bacteria, are made up of only one cell.

Scientists who study cells and other tiny living things are called microbiologists. Biology is the study of life, and "micro" comes from a Greek word that means "small." One of the first microbiologists was a British man named Robert Hooke. He was the person who first gave cells their name in 1665.

Fast Fact

Cells are so tiny that scientists must measure them in units of measurement called micrometers. A micrometer is equal to 0.000039 inch. A human cell is about 20 micrometers (0.00078 in) across. It would take about 10,000 human cells to cover the head of a pin!

Two Kinds of Cells

Scientists divide living things with cells into two main groups: prokaryotes and eukaryotes. Prokaryotes include bacteria and other small organisms called archaea. Plants, fungi, and animals—including humans—are eukaryotes. A eukaryotic cell is often just part of a larger

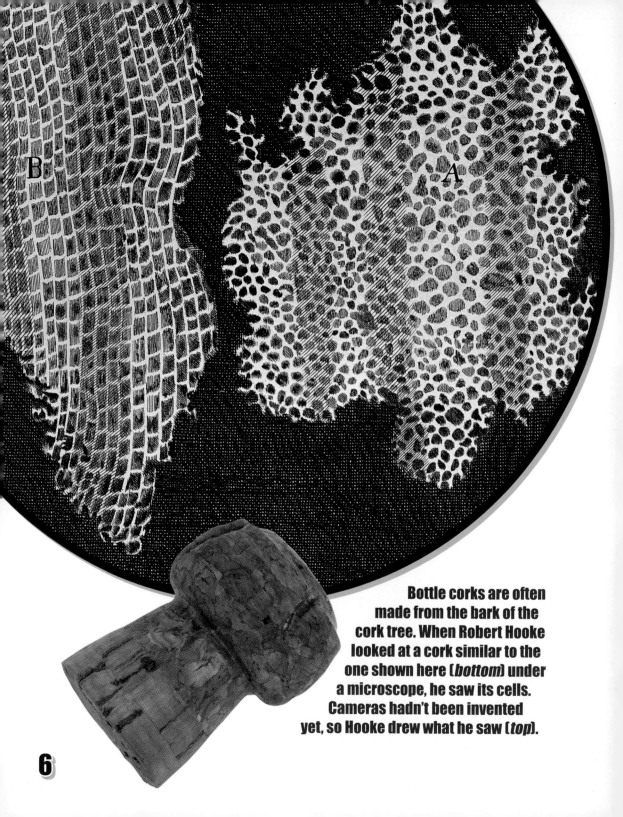

A

B

Bottle corks are often made from the bark of the cork tree. When Robert Hooke looked at a cork similar to the one shown here (*bottom*) under a microscope, he saw its cells. Cameras hadn't been invented yet, so Hooke drew what he saw (*top*).

organism, but a prokaryotic cell is the entire organism. Prokaryotes are also called single-celled (sometimes called unicellular) organisms. The most common unicellular organisms are the most common organisms on Earth—bacteria.

While eukaryotic cells are more complex than prokaryotic cells, their basic structure is similar. All cells have a surrounding casing called the cell

Many archaea are extremophiles, which means they can live in places that would kill most other creatures. For example, they can be found in the superheated waters of the Norris Geyser at Yellowstone National Park.

Fast Fact

When scientists first discovered archaea in the 1970s, they thought they were bacteria. Today, we know they're completely different organisms. In fact, they're more like us than they are like bacteria!

OUTER LAYERS

The cell membrane holds the cell together and controls what can enter it. You can think of it as the "skin" of the cell. Cells couldn't exist without it. Some kinds of cells also have an extra, stiff outer layer called a cell wall. This adds extra protection and support.

All plant cells have a cell wall, but no animal cells do. This is because of the stiffness of the cell wall. In plants, it's helpful; it keeps them standing upright toward the sun. In animals, it would be harmful. If all your cells had walls, you'd be as stiff as a tree!

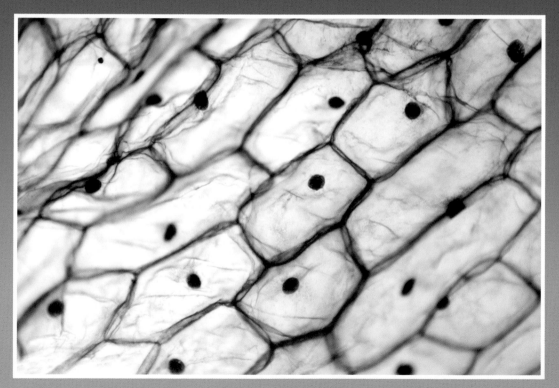

The dark purple lines in this microscopic photo of an onion are the walls of the onion cells.

membrane that holds in the cell's other parts. They're filled with fluid, and most contain genetic material called deoxyribonucleic acid (DNA). Prokaryotic and eukaryotic cells do most of the same things, including dividing to create more cells and getting rid of waste.

Major Differences

Prokaryotic and eukaryotic cells look different under a microscope, especially if you know what to look for. For example, a key way to tell the difference between eukaryotic and prokaryotic cells under a microscope is finding their genetic material. Eukaryotic cells have a **nucleus** surrounded by a membrane. Prokaryotes don't. Instead, their genetic material floats around in a part of the cell called the nucleoid. Prokaryotes are also shaped differently than eukaryotes. The three main shapes of prokaryotes are spheres, or circular shapes; rods, or long, thin shapes; and spirals, or twisted shapes.

Another major difference between prokaryotes and eukaryotes is how they relate to each other. Bacteria cells may live together in a group called a colony. However, each of these cells operates independently. Eukaryotic cells often work together within an organism. They may differentiate— or become different kinds of cells— as they grow. This is why people have skin cells, muscle cells, bone cells, and more. All these cells work together to make up the human body.

Fast Fact

Viruses are neither prokaryotes nor eukaryotes. They're bits of DNA that can reproduce only through living cells. Scientists disagree about whether we should call viruses living things or not.

CILIA

BACK AND FRONT BEATING

FLAGELLA

PROPELLER-LIKE MOTION

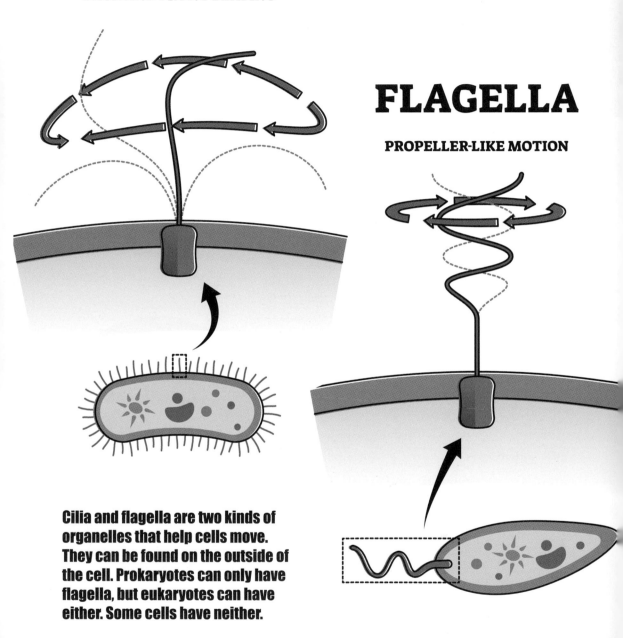

Cilia and flagella are two kinds of organelles that help cells move. They can be found on the outside of the cell. Prokaryotes can only have flagella, but eukaryotes can have either. Some cells have neither.

INSIDE CELLS

Inside animal bodies, including humans, there are organs that are needed to keep the body alive and working properly. These include the heart, stomach, liver, lungs, and much more. Inside cells, there are organelles—a word that means "little organs." Organelles can do things such as help the cell move, store DNA, and create energy to keep the cell going.

Protecting the Cell

Any cell's first line of defense is its outer membrane. It's made of **proteins** and fats. In addition to building cell membranes, these fats are an important way organisms store energy. The membrane allows needed matter into the cell and keeps harmful matter out. Cell waste also moves out through the membrane.

In the complex eukaryotic cells, organelles are also surrounded by membranes. The only organelle the simple prokaryotes have is ribosomes, which aren't surrounded by a membrane in either kind of

Fast Fact

Scientists believe there are more bacteria in your body than there are human cells! Most of these prokaryotes live in the stomach and intestines. Without them, we wouldn't be able to break down food.

11

cell. You can think of this like rooms in a house. In a eukaryotic cell, the membranes are like the walls and doors that separate rooms in a house. In a prokaryotic cell, everything is open. There are no walls except around the outside, and things move around freely inside.

A prokaryotic cell is a little like this home. Instead of separate rooms for the kitchen and bedroom, it's all in one big room.

Fast Fact

Prokaryotes were the first form of life on Earth. Today, 3.5-billion-year-old stromatolites—layers of rock formed by the growth of **cyanobacteria**—can still be found in some parts of the ocean, especially near the Australian coast.

Types of Organelles

Depending on what kind it is, a cell may contain several organelles to carry out important functions.

- Ribosomes make the proteins that keep the cell running smoothly. Different kinds of proteins help cells keep their shape, remove waste, receive signals from outside the cell, and much more.
- The endoplasmic reticulum (ER) moves molecules around the cell. Some parts of the ER have ribosomes attached to them. The ER sends the proteins that the ribosomes make to the Golgi apparatus.
- The Golgi apparatus acts much like a post office. It takes the proteins the ER sends it and transports them to the parts of the cell where they're needed. All eukaryotes have at least one Golgi apparatus, and some—mainly plant cells—can have hundreds.

The Golgi apparatus is named after the scientist who discovered it, Camillo Golgi. "Apparatus" is a word that means "a complicated device."

Prokaryotic

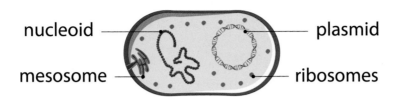

nucleoid —— plasmid

mesosome —— ribosomes

Eukaryotic

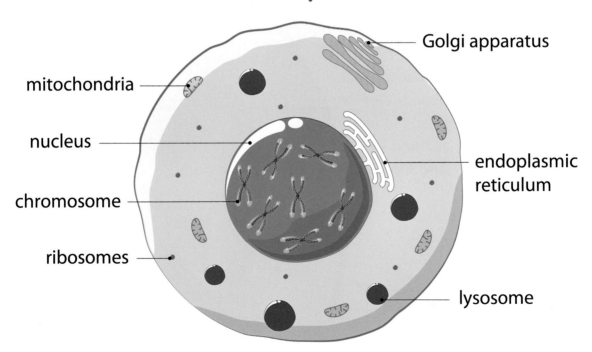

Golgi apparatus

mitochondria

nucleus

endoplasmic reticulum

chromosome

ribosomes

lysosome

This picture shows the differences between a prokaryotic cell and a eukaryotic cell.

CELL ENERGY

Did you know that the energy you get from your food comes from processes in cells? Eukaryotic cells use organelles called mitochondria to break down glucose, a kind of sugar you get from food. Glucose is then changed into energy. Mitochondria have an outer membrane that encloses them and a folded inner membrane too. They also have a small bit of special DNA that helps them make proteins.

In addition to mitochondria, plant cells have energy-producing organelles called chloroplasts. These structures use photosynthesis, a process that changes sunlight, carbon dioxide, and water to energy, rather than breaking down food.

- Lysosomes are structures with special materials called enzymes that break down molecules into waste, including damaged organelles or bacteria that enter the cell.
- Vacuoles and vesicles are organelles that are used for storage and chemical movement. Plant cells have a much larger, central vacuole than animal cells, which have several small ones.

Fast Fact

Since prokaryotes don't have mitochondria or chloroplasts, they use a simple process called glycolysis to break down food and make energy. Eukaryotes can carry out glycolysis too.

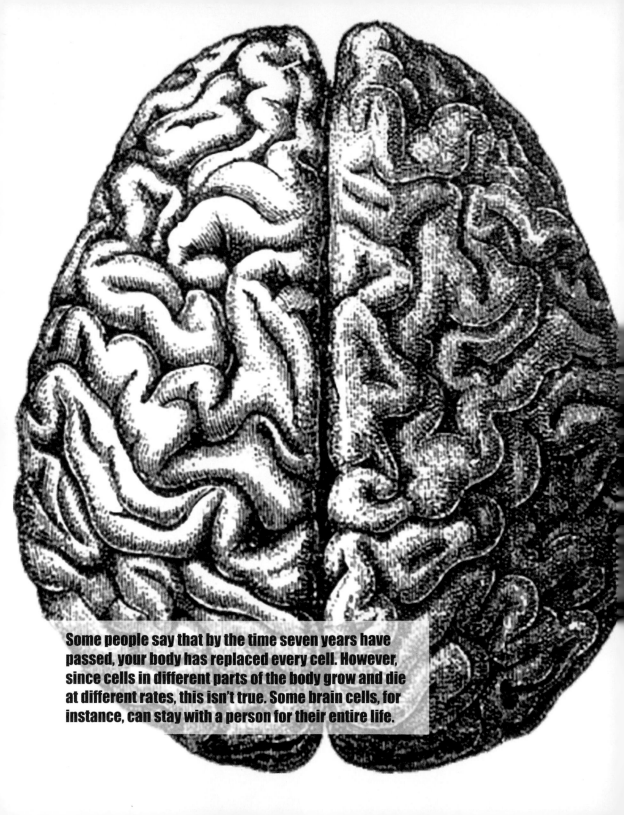

Some people say that by the time seven years have passed, your body has replaced every cell. However, since cells in different parts of the body grow and die at different rates, this isn't true. Some brain cells, for instance, can stay with a person for their entire life.

Chapter Three

LIFE AND DEATH

Because cells are living things, they also die. In a human body, when cells die, they're removed, and new ones take their place. Sometimes you notice this, and sometimes you don't. For example, if you've ever had dry, flaky skin, you've seen dead skin cells. You don't see the cells inside your body being removed and replaced, but it happens all the time.

Specialized Cells

When a baby is created, it starts as one cell, which we call a zygote. Although a zygote is alive just like any other cell, it isn't a living human yet. The zygote divides over and over again—one cell becomes two, those two become four, those four become eight, and so on. After about eight weeks, the cells have differentiated, or turned into different kinds of cells that do specialized work. Parts of a cell's DNA are turned

> **Fast Fact**
>
> Everything in a human body is made of cells, including your hair. However, your hair cells die after they grow past your scalp. That's why it hurts to pull a hair out of your head, but not to get your hair cut.

This photo, taken under a microscope, shows a human embryo, which develops after the zygote begins dividing.

"on" or "off" to make it become part of a kidney, leg bone, skin, or other body part. Cells then specialize further. Even among one tissue or organ's specialized cells, there must be different cells to perform the work of each part. The cells from your different body parts look a little bit different from each other under a microscope.

In an embryo, which is a stage of life that comes after the zygote starts to divide, every kind of cell starts off looking the same

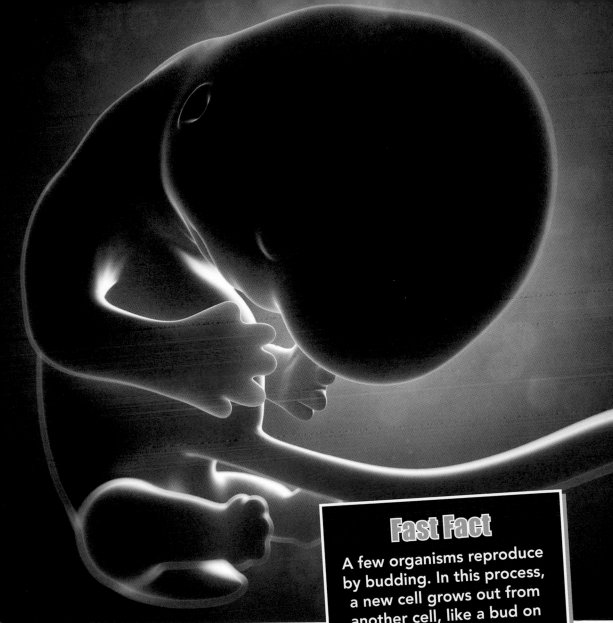

After eight weeks, the embryo has become what we call a fetus. It still can't live outside the mother's body on its own, but it looks more like a baby than an embryo does.

Fast Fact

A few organisms reproduce by budding. In this process, a new cell grows out from another cell, like a bud on a tree. After the bud is formed, DNA is copied and passed into it. Then, the bud splits off to become its own cell.

DEATH OF A CELL

If a cell is damaged or infected, it may allow itself to die. Cell death is called apoptosis. Apoptosis is an important cell process since it stops cells that aren't working properly from dividing and creating more unhealthy cells. Cells can also be killed. For example, when you stay in the sun too long, you may kill your skin cells. We call that sunburn!

When apoptosis doesn't happen, the uncontrolled cell division causes a disease called cancer. Cancerous cell growth starts with a single cell that has damaged DNA. Usually, the kind of DNA damage that causes healthy cells to become cancer cells takes a long time to happen.

before it differentiates. These are called stem cells. As they grow, stem cells change into whatever the body needs them to be. Once they've differentiated, they don't change again; your blood cells can't turn into skin cells when the old skin cells die. Instead, other cells divide to replace them. Adults have a small number of stem cells that their body can use when it needs to, but these can't change into as many different kinds of cells as embryonic stem cells can.

The Importance of Division

Cell division is important to the survival of all kinds of organisms. In unicellular organisms, cell division creates more of that kind of

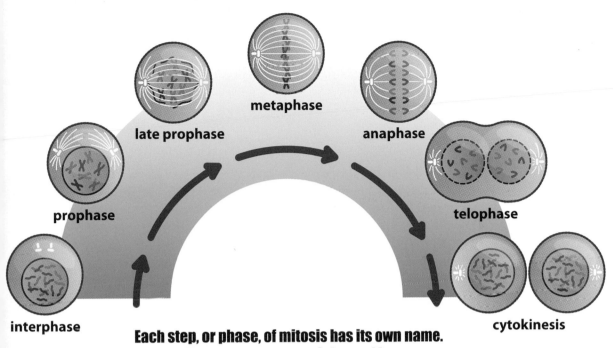

metaphase

late prophase

anaphase

prophase

telophase

interphase

cytokinesis

Each step, or phase, of mitosis has its own name. These names are mainly used by biologists who grow and study cells.

organism. In other words, that's how bacteria and archaea have "babies." Healthy cell division also helps multicellular organisms grow and repair themselves.

Most prokaryotes reproduce by binary fission. In eukaryotes, this process is called mitosis. In both binary fission and mitosis, the cell first makes a copy of its DNA. Then it splits in two with one copy of the DNA in each cell.

In the human body, the only cells that can't divide are red blood cells. This is because they don't have a nucleus. Their job is to carry oxygen throughout the body, so losing the nucleus leaves more room for oxygen in the cell. Instead of undergoing mitosis, stem cells in the bones create more red blood cells over time. It takes about two days to make one red blood cell.

Human cells are more than 70 percent water.
Drinking water helps keep them working properly.

Chapter Four

WHAT CAN CELLS TEACH US?

Understanding cells isn't important only for biologists. Since cells keep our bodies working, we all need to know about them. Everything we eat or drink—and some things we touch or smell, as well—affects our cells. Knowing how cells work and how things affect them helps us make healthy choices.

Fast Fact

Identical twins are formed when one embryo splits into two separate babies. Fraternal twins are formed when two different embryos form inside a mother. Identical twins have identical DNA; fraternal twins don't.

Human DNA

The DNA inside human cells controls just about everything about us, from our eye color to whether we like the taste of Brussels sprouts. In 1953, scientists James Watson and Francis Crick made a model of human DNA. The shape of DNA is called a "double helix." A helix is a 3-D spiral shape, like a corkscrew. DNA looks like two of those put together. The double helix helped explain how our DNA copies itself to make more DNA. The order in which

DNA
DEOXYRIBONUCLEIC ACID

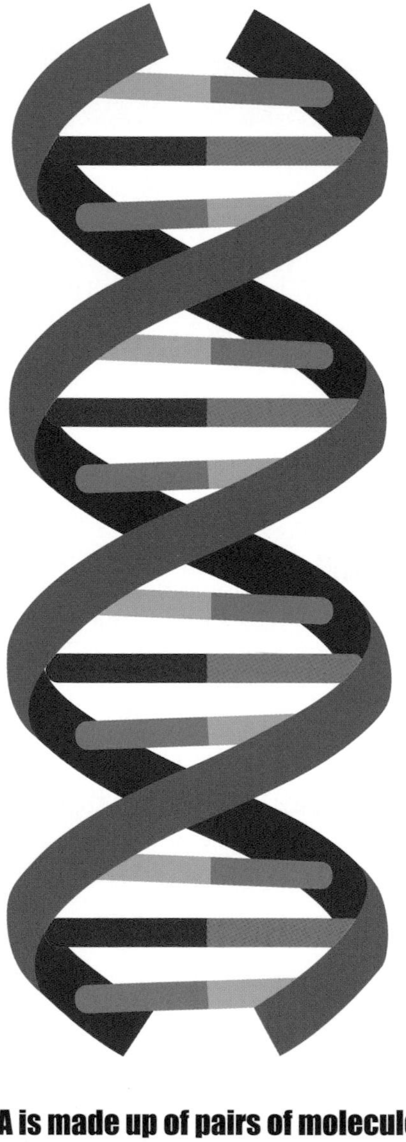

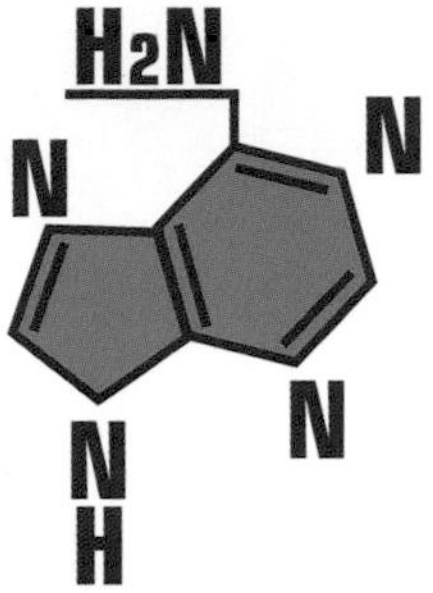

ADENINE

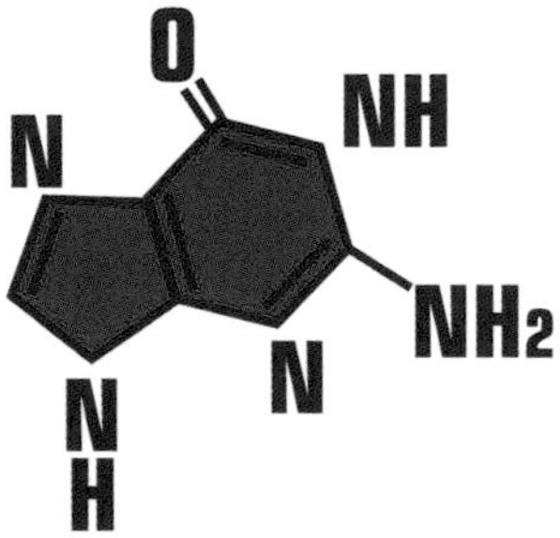

GUANINE

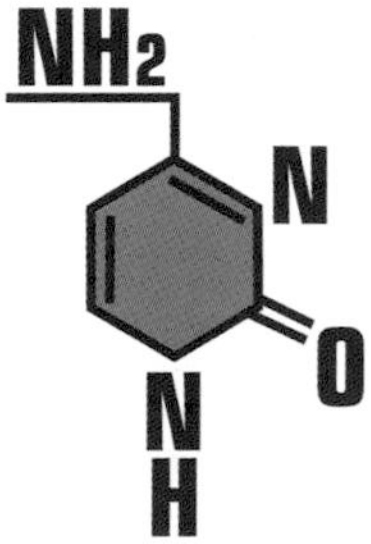

CYTOSINE

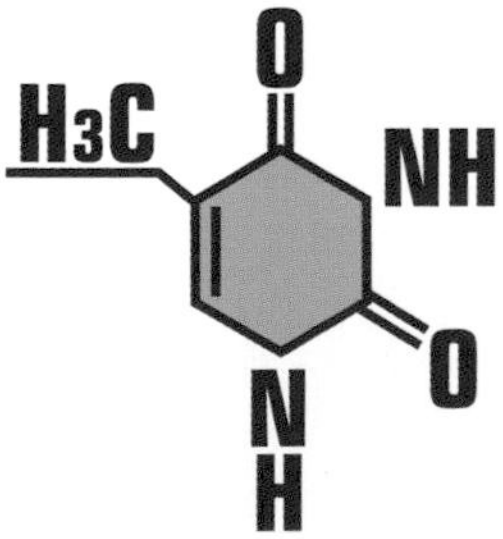

THYMINE

DNA is made up of pairs of molecules. These pairs can appear in different orders on a string of DNA, and that order is the code that tells our cells what to do.

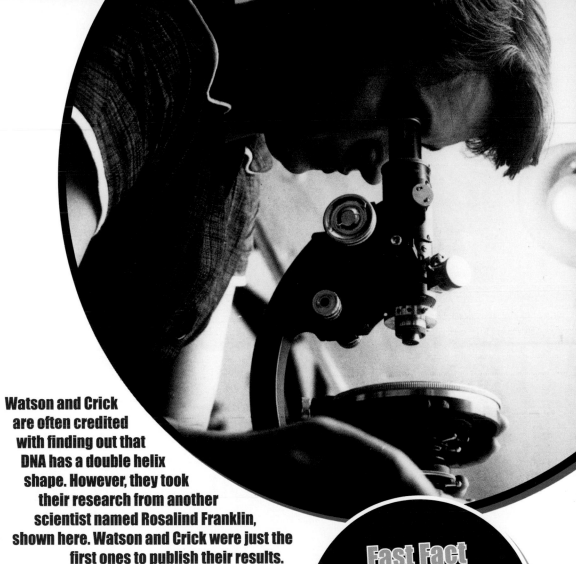

Watson and Crick are often credited with finding out that DNA has a double helix shape. However, they took their research from another scientist named Rosalind Franklin, shown here. Watson and Crick were just the first ones to publish their results.

the DNA molecules appear is a code that tells a cell what to do. Even the smallest change to the order—for example, if three pairs of adenine and thymine appear in a row instead of just two—can change the code completely.

Fast Fact

Some people believe that things we take into our body, such as vaccines or certain kinds of food, can change our DNA. However, this is impossible.

CELLS IN SPACE

Astronauts are scientists who work in space. One kind of experiment they do is looking at how cells behave in space. This helps them learn more about how cells work on Earth. One ambitious experiment performed by NASA was called the Twins Study. It involved identical twin astronauts Mark and Scott Kelly. From 2015 to 2016, Scott lived on the International Space Station (ISS), and Mark stayed on Earth.

The Twins Study showed that living in space can make big changes to our cells, including some things about our DNA. These findings will help scientists prepare for a long spaceflight, such as a manned mission to Mars.

The Kelly twins, Mark (*left*) and Scott (*right*), helped NASA learn a lot about the human body both in space and on Earth.

Cells Under the Microscope

As microscopes have improved over the years, so has our knowledge of cells. The very first microscopes in the 1660s weren't much more powerful than a magnifying glass, but they were enough to let scientists see bacteria as well as plant and animal cells. By the 1880s, microscopes were powerful enough to let scientists start seeing organelles. However, they still couldn't see them very well, so it took a while to figure out what they all did. For example, even though scientists first saw mitochondria in 1840, they didn't figure out that they provide energy to the cell until 1890.

The kind of microscope most classrooms have can only see relatively large cell features, such as the cell wall, cell membrane, nucleus, and chloroplasts in plant cells. These are **optical** microscopes, and they use light to see the **specimen**. In biology labs, scientists have much stronger microscopes called **electron** microscopes. However, the problem with electron microscopes is that they can't look at living cells in action, only dead cells. This lets scientists see organelles in a lot of detail, but not how the organelles work.

In 2011, a group of scientists in England started using an optical microscope powerful enough to study the parts of a human cell. It's called the microsphere nanoscope, and it allows scientists to see the parts of a cell in great detail while the cell is still living. This has taught scientists things about cells they could only guess at in the past. As scientific instruments continue to improve, we will likely learn a lot more about the world around us—and our own bodies—in the future.

Fast Fact

When using most optical microscopes, scientists need ways to make details of a cell stand out so they can see them more clearly. One way to do this is to stain, or dye, a specimen.

THINK ABOUT IT!

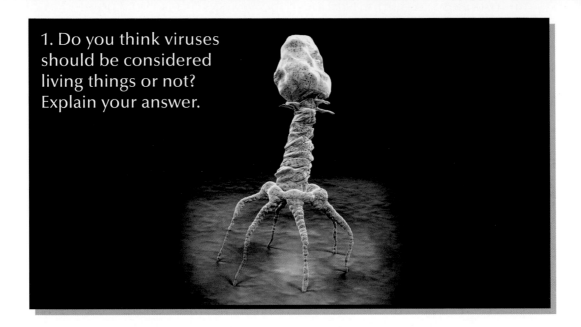

1. Do you think viruses should be considered living things or not? Explain your answer.

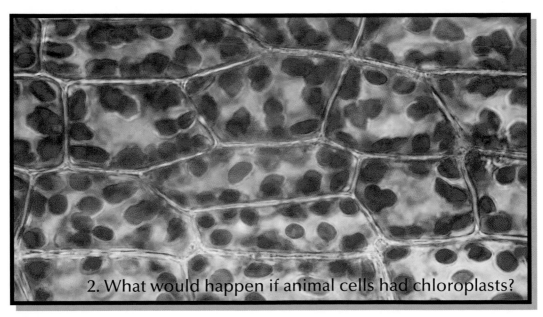

2. What would happen if animal cells had chloroplasts?

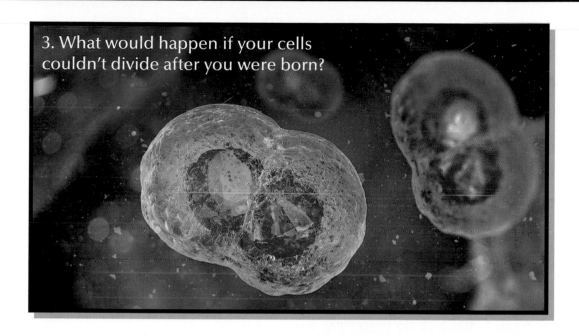

3. What would happen if your cells couldn't divide after you were born?

4. Aside from drinking water, what are some things that are healthy or unhealthy for your cells?

GLOSSARY

complex: Having many parts, details, ideas, or functions often related in a complicated way.

cyanobacteria: A type of photosynthetic bacteria, also called blue-green algae, that form colonies in water, soil, and rocks.

electron: A tiny particle in atoms that has a negative charge.

membrane: A thin, soft, flexible sheet or layer, especially of a plant or animal part.

nucleus: A eukaryotic cell part that is necessary for heredity and for making proteins, that contains the chromosomes, and that is enclosed in a nuclear membrane.

optical: Having to do with light and vision.

proteins: Long chains of molecules called amino acids that are needed to keep living things alive.

specimen: A sample of a group.

Books

Bunting, Philip. *Me, Microbes & I.* Victoria, Australia: Little Hare, 2021.

Fisher, Carolyn. *Cells: An Owner's Handbook.* New York, NY: Beach Lane Books, 2019.

McKenzie, Precious. *The Micro World of Plant and Animal Cells.* North Mankato, MN: Capstone Press, 2022.

Websites

BrainPOP: Cells
www.brainpop.com/science/freemovies/cells
Watch a movie and play games to learn more about different kinds of cells.

Coolaboo: Cell Organelles
www.coolaboo.com/biology/cell-organelles
Learn about the differences between plant and animal cells, and take a quiz to test your knowledge.

Ducksters: The Cell
www.ducksters.com/science/the_cell.php
Read more cool facts about cells and their organelles.

Publisher's note to educators and parents: Our editors have carefully reviewed these websites to ensure that they are suitable for students. Many websites change frequently, however, and we cannot guarantee that a site's future contents will continue to meet our high standards of quality and educational value. Be advised that students should be closely supervised whenever they access the internet.

INDEX